The universe exists in a very delicate balance. Disturb it and your world will be destroyed. An Ancient Text.

2017-2020

Life is full of small things. If you miss the small things you miss life.

2017-2020

"Intelligent people use their minds. Nature therefore creates fools so that the world can move on."

2017-2020

Just hours before the Titanic sank the sailors were excited at being in such an engineering marvel of its time.

2017-2020

"What you get is intricately linked to how the globe is doing. It's therefore your business to know about the globe."

2016: Trump - The presidential candidate: A guarantee for market mayhem. A Dow Jones nightmare.

Mar 2016: Credit Suisse announced that it plans to fire 6000 of its employees.

Mar 2016: A steel major announced exit from Britain. 15,000 jobs on the line...40,000 more jobs affected.

Oct 2016: Deutsche Bank stock touches single digit. 9000 jobs on the line.

Nov 2016: Iconic Marks And Spencer - Shuts Down 10,20,30,40,50,60,70,80,90... 100 Stores.

Nov 2016: France Prime Minister "Europe On Brink Of Collapse."

Nov 2016: Trump Elected President of America: A Dow Dream Run. The 'Messiah' of American business is born.

Dec 2016: The same steel major announced NO EXIT from Britain. 15,000 jobs saved. 40,000 more jobs affected positively.

Feb 2017: Toshiba Nuclear (US) faces bankruptcy.

Feb 2017: Dow At All Time High.

Jan 2017: Trump wades into South China Sea.

Feb 2017: China tests a Dragon. A missile with 10 nuclear war heads. The world takes another step towards danger.

It's Right Here, Facing You.

THE UNPREDICTABLE FUTURE.

Fast, Quick, Volatile, Tectonic.

Changes Before You Can Grasp What Is Happening.

How Then Do You React?

How Then Do You Invest? How Do You Secure Yourself?

4

2017 – 2020

The Unpredictable Future.

"What you get is intricately linked to how the globe is doing. It's therefore your business to know about the globe."

COPYRIGHT@DR.RAVINHUMBARWADI

PIAM CREATIONS

Reach Out To Me: pi.con.publisher@gmail.com

IT'S NOT JUST TRUMP

Sometime in 1930, Herbert Hoover signed the tariff that started a global trade war. That trade war led to the most 'famous' depression of all time.

Now Trump is talking tariffs. That will make Chinese (the China low cost tariff) and Mexico (the Mexico wall tariff) and other targeted countries' products expensive. In retaliation, these targeted countries may stop buying American products from aerospace to All American brands. And USA will be right in the center of the Great Trade War of the 22nd century.

The future now is intricately linked to Trump and his decisions. The Dow has believed in him and is at an all-time high. So also the national debt. USA 20 trillion. I can actually visualize the media screaming headlines in Feb-Mar 2017 when the American debt hits a historic $ 20 trillion mark.

Will one man do it for you all? Will he deliver?

What if he does? What if he doesn't? I don't need to tell you. You very well know that 2017 and the coming couple of years can have extreme swings before we can even make sense of what is happening. Is there a middle ground? Of course. Something positive and something negative, not here-not there, like it has been. So, this adds another dimension to the already convoluted scenario.

It's not just Trump. It's the entire globe that's topsy-turvy.

We are in the third largest expansion in the history of capitalism. Every expansion has had an end and this one will too. One of the longest in recent memories which started in the 1990's ended in surprise dot com bust.

We all know at the back of our minds that 'Good times must come to an end after all.'

The triggers are many - the possible trade war, the big bank mess of Europe, the stagnation of Japan, the inertia of China, the outcome of easy money now being converted to tight money, the polarization of the world, and the explosive South China Sea – North Korea.

Many other unpredictable situations and unpleasant situations abound.

On February 11 2016 Janet Yellen chaired a meet of the US Federal Reserve. During the meet, news channels were abuzz - 'China faced its worst year of economic growth in a quarter century. Oil went down again putting a question mark on the oil centric economies of Russia, Brazil and the Middle East. Wall Street closed to the worst ever start to a year.'

Gold spiked. The safe haven.

But then, there was a $100-$200 downslide in gold around the Dec-2016 Fed rate hike. Would gold tank below $1000 when Fed again increases the rates multiple times in 2017. Safe haven no longer. Corporate America is on a Trump mania. If Trump delivers, gold may well go down. Jitters. If expectations are belied will America be pushed into a recession in late 2017? Then perhaps gold will have a record spike. Jitters again.

The future. It's unpredictable.

But then we have the perfect plan — The 2017-2020 Investment Strategy — Hedged for a Downturn and Positioned to Ride A Wave.

We have added options you might not even have thought of. But then unique situations call for novel ideas. And we believe tough situations can be an adventure if we are ready for it.

Are you ready? For the adventure of your life? Because the unpredictable future is here.

Feb 2016

News: Stocks are down in the dumps the world over. It was a catastrophic night. And going by the early signs, it won't be a pretty morning as markets are sliding again...

News: Worldwide stocks stumbled on fears over the health of the global economy. The global equity benchmark index closed more than 20 per cent below its record high in 2015. An all-country world equity index, which tracked shares in 45 nations hit its lowest level in more than two and a half years.

Were the actions of the political class and the central banks the answer to combat the 2008 recession? Let's have a quick check of our finances!

China, USA, Europe, Japan and Middle East. Let's journey.

The Great Fall Of China

Let's begin with China. Because this is where it all began.

Problems arising from China have globally crashed stock and commodity markets in early 2016.

The iron ore that China gulped from Rio de Janeiro to Australia was used to build mega fetal cities. The 'fetal - unborn cities' that became infamous across the globe as the 'ghost cities of China'. The world's second biggest economy built cities after cities, hundreds of them but not a single person chose to stay.

Unborn, unused and unusable. Homes, restaurants, malls, gladiatorial stadia that should have been bustling with vibrant people were mute witness to empty space.

It took some time before the world became aware of this. It seemed more fictional than truth.

China's 'infrastructure' driven growth of two decades costed billions and led to a cascading worldwide boom starting off with commodity prices.

Were the 'unborn cities' at the core of this global boom?

Tremendous money had gone in but resulted in no output making these the debt cities of China.

The showpiece of an economic boom was just dead weight in the sinking ship of China and the global economy.

Somewhere the cities had to stop because they were lying empty.

And when it did the commodities that went into the making of the cities crashed. As much as 50 % - 80% and more.

The debt was funded by bonds, many of which were collateralized with copper. And copper was down. So neither was there a ROI nor was there value in the collateral. Debt recovery was a distant dream.

More the debt, more the trouble. We all want to hide our debts. But sooner or later it will come out in the open. Then all mayhem breaks loose. Like it did in Feb 2016.

The Chinese economy is posting its slowest rate since 1990. China's forex reserves are down by a whopping 1 trillion dollars.

The Chinese manufacturing PMI revealed a sluggish industrial production for 10 consecutive months. No wonder then, in Feb 2016 the Chinese equity markets went into a downslide.

Marc Faber, the author of 'Gloom and Doom Report' says that 'the Chinese economy was heading for a hard-landing, as borrowers piled up debt and were finding it difficult to pay interest.'

George Soros stated that the current Chinese situation "amounts to a crisis" and brings memories of the recession of 2008. "China is struggling to find a new growth model and its currency devaluation is transferring problems to the rest of the world."

China was releasing huge cash into its financial system in an effort to stem the tide. But you cannot treat a cancer with a placebo.

The Chinese feared a quick devaluation of their currency.

The last time China devalued Renminbi, it caused the Asian currency crisis.

China challenged a currency trader. Not to bet against the Renminbi.

George Soros may be legendary.

Yet you are left with a niggling thought: The mighty colossus challenges a mere trader! Why should a colossus even acknowledge let alone take cognizance of a trader of currencies?

14   Because the Chinese bureaucrats are clueless. China is unfolding and they don't know what to do.

The tiger seems to have grown

It and the world knows the great days of the economy are just a fading memory. It's scary, even for China.

As of October 2016 the credit to GDP gap was at 30%. 10% is the highest as per international norms.

'China is in the midst of a triple bubble, with the third-largest credit bubble of all time, the largest investment bubble and the second-largest real-estate bubble.' This is a Credit Suisse analysis.

In 1992, George Soros became known as the man who "broke" the Bank of England. He gained $1 billion betting that the pound would collapse.

What do you think George Soros has done in 2016?

He has bet against Asian currencies and commodity linked economies.

Now, one Mr. Donald Trump is the President of USA.

However much you may or may not revile Trump some of his opinions are cruelly or even breathtakingly true. He seems to be the only one capable of taking the bull by the horns. But as he brings up trade to the table the issues will only spiral.

Ding Deng.

China Is Unfolding. Stay Alert.

USA Uncertain

Feb 11 2016. Janet Yellen at a Fed meet accepted that if the recent dire global economic indicators continued it could be multiplying downside risk to the USA.

The unemployed and the not so well employed number in the USA was an election issue and these formed the swell of support to Trump, the unlikely candidate. This was well known. Americans in large numbers did not have enough savings in their bank account.

What was the reason for this situation that USA found itself in?

There were three rounds of quantitative easing (QE).

QE1 was from 2008 to 2010. The US Fed bought $2.1 trillion of treasury bonds and mortgage-backed securities. This stopped when the Fed indicated that there was improvement in the economy.

But the recovery proved to be false.

So QE 2 was on. It started in November 2010 and lasted till the middle of 2011. During QE2 the US Fed bought $600 billion of bonds comprising mostly mortgage-backed securities.

After a little more than a year the Fed realized there was no real recovery.

So it started QE3 in late 2012 and during this program the Fed pumped in $85billion per month. The Fed began reducing those purchases at the start of 2015.

The Fed has spent more than $4trillion in buying bonds.

There is a broad consensus that QE1 was a success - it was quite big: a couple of trillion dollars, and lasted quite long: a couple of years. It helped in preventing the 2008 recession becoming worse than it was.

QE2 was only a third as effective as QE1. The San Francisco Federal Reserve Bank, found that QE2 added just 0.13 percentage points to the annual rate of economic growth in 2010, which was at 2.8% when the program was implemented.

The Fed had a prolonged QE3. And it would prove to be the unwanted QE. The QE that did the damage. The QE that disrupted the caravan.

Money at low rates leads to speculation. It would be a fallacy to think that highs of the US stock markets are not in large measure due to the QE.

Now that the QE is not there that much of easy investment that pushed up stocks is off the market.

Andrew, a former manager of the Fed's mortgage-buying scheme, has commented that low rates may not have helped ordinary Americans.

Was Wall Street sucking in most of the extra cash?

Greed. The greed of Wall Street. But then a cardinal sin never goes without leaving a trail and retribution. Does it?

Printing money in the world's biggest economy also had an impact on global economies.

The European Central Bank, found that QE1 and QE2 led to spillovers in as many as 65 economies across the globe.

The study revealed that QE1 led investors to invest in USA while QE2 led investment into emerging economies. Now, that source of easy money is shut and scores of countries are feeling the 'Easy Money Withdrawal Syndrome.' The tap is dry and they are feeling blanked out.

A lot of Americans want Donald Trump as their president. An almost equal number want him in the top position in the world. Would he have had this support if the situation had been different? Terrorism apart, has not the state of the economy led a large section of the people to look towards someone like Trump to spruce up the system in Washington?

Hillary Clinton may have been the bettor's choice but Trump is a creation of his times. And creation of the times however eccentric have been known to be unusually powerful.

Ben Bernanke spent $3 trillion to make the NYSE a bull market for half a dozen years. Janet Yellen hiked the interest rate by a quarter point and the bull market tanked by a third of its value.

In September 2016 the Fed once again postponed the itsy bitsy rate hike. It looked so huge, so gargantuan. Given the weak signals continuing to emanate from the economy.

The fragile economy has left no one bold enough to bite the bullet.

"The world is an uncertain place, and all monetary policymakers can really be sure of is that what will happen is often different from what we currently expect." Stanley Fischer, the No. 2 at the U.S. Federal Reserve.

Trump was seen as the enemy by mainstream corporate America for the entire time he was the presidential candidate. No Fortune 100 CEO contributed to the Trump campaign.

USA was Uncertain…

Till one day. The day the world woke up, astonished to see their nightmare come live on television. The sight of Donald Trump the 'monster' giving his acceptance speech.

Gold moved as much up as down in a single day. The Dow went crazy.

And suddenly corporate USA became certain. 'We have a great future.'

Donald Trump appeared so humble in victory, so accommodating and so sensible.

Just in the course of a day the monster of the Dow became a darling of the Dow.

It was absolutely unpredictable.

The Dow still keeps breaking records. But the best time to book profits is fast approaching.

USA Uncertain to Unpredictable...

Europe Lives In Delusion

Feb 2016 News: 'SocGen leads European banks lower at the close as Deutsche, Barclays, HSBC, Lloyds and RBS share prices fall.'

Europe's top banks were down in the dumps. And still are. And that is putting the case lightly. Deutsche Bank's share went down lower than its recession price. Standard Chartered's share price is at its lowest in nearly 20 years.

The Swiss Bank Credit Suisse stock was down 43 percent over the last year and touched a 27-year low. If Credit Suisse tried to sell their bonds they would get junk rates in 2016. Their trading income was abysmal.

In UK, HSBC, Lloyds, Barclays and RBS tell a similar story.

Falling off a cliff. Since the beginning of 2016, the Stoxx Europe 600 Banks Index, had lost 27 per cent.

If you had invested in banks a decade ago you would have not made a profit. That was in Feb 2016. By Nov 2016 you would have made a loss.

After 2008 the economy in developed countries was not exciting. So banks turned to emerging Asian and African economies providing them eight years of easy money.

Now, increasingly, borrowers in millions don't have the money to repay.

The problem with banks is — they ask you to take a loan and then they want you to pay it back whether you have the money or not.

Was there any forecast. Any sort of analysis? Could the banks not even foresee the effect of providing money at a flow? Is it a bubble waiting to burst in Europe?

Watch Deutsche stock price reach single digit. Pathetic.

The credit default swap (CDS) of Deutsche has risen to high levels. This means that the cost of insuring against a default by Deutsche has risen considerably.

Flashback 2008: Remember the banks which fell. Some of them never got up. Be careful which bank you put your money.

The moon is a safe place. There are no banks on the moon.

They will drive you mad, the banks. If banks go down, they will take everything else with them.

Why does common sense get the kick when it comes to managing global economy?

The European Central Bank (ECB) increases its very own quantitative easing, piling on public debt to the private debt it has already accumulated. The ECB has planned to increase its QE from €14 billion to €60 billion until at least September of 2016.

It has failed in US. It has failed in Japan. Still the ECB is at it. It will act as a multiplier of economic dangers. But then perhaps ECB has no other option.

The more you blow a bubble the bigger it gets. The bigger a bubble balloon the louder it will burst.

ECB is blowing the cash bubble. More and more. Harder and harder.

It's all about the banks in Europe. Seven of the top 10 distressed banks are in Europe. Monte Paschi of Italy, Deutsche of Germany are all over the news, their desperate attempts to stay afloat is now so common it does not seem out of place.

"A bad bank in Europe? Ah! Tell me something excitin'."

The US Justice department has sent out a notice for $ 14 billion fine in a case of mortgage security sale fraud. And the market value of Deutsche bank is only 16 billion dollars. It holds less than 3% of assets as capital.

A quagmire of banks in a cesspool.

Nov 2016: French PM 'Europe on the brink of collapse.'

Add to that the Exit and other potential Exits. The bankrupt countries and countries on the verge of bankruptcy.

Europe Lives In Delusion...

The Gulf Deficit

Oil. It seems fantasy that oil was more than 100 dollars just a couple of years back. When it touched 40 the venerable sheiks wished that was the bottom.

They survive on oil. And oil will never bounce back to those heady days.

The technology for drilling is making the cost of drilling out oil lesser and lesser.

Moreover, the era of oil is over. Done and oiled.

Humanity has to look ahead, look elsewhere. One day or the other, oil had to be exhausted. We discovered engines and invented modern ways to use oil just a 100 - 150 years ago. In the span of human history this is like a blip click. But we have used oil as much as we could and overheated the globe in the process. Life is transient. Hard luck.

In 2015, its budget deficit nearly reached $ 100 billion. Now, Saudi Arabia is looking for an $8 billion loan. Headcounts are being lowered. Cost cutting which was once unthinkable in the gulf countries is becoming policy.

In 2016 six of the rich Arab economies planned to borrow upto $20 billion. Till now they were the lenders to the world. Now they are planned borrowers. This is the state of affairs when oil touched 40.

And these have nil else to prop their economy as of now. The venerable sheiks have put all their eggs in the oil basket.

It is only now they have realized this and are making attempts to diversify. But that will take time to happen.

After a long fight within themselves the OPEC has finally in Oct 2016 agreed to decrease oil output by a million barrels a day. It is a bit of an upside for oil prices and to their economies. From 33 million barrels a day to 32 million barrels a day. And just 2 weeks later the entire agreement has come unhinged. There is a see-saw among the OPEC members. Russia, a non-OPEC member has increased its output and agrees for a freeze. No decrease from Russia, only a freeze at current levels. So this drama to keep oil rates high enough continues.

In the longer term, oil is an exhaustible energy source. Alternative energies are the future of civilization.

Governments the world over are promoting alternative energies. Technology is gaining. We have had Solar Impulse make a round the world trip with not a drop of gasoline. West Asia the hub of oil and gas has itself been making a shift to solar energy production lately.

Countries have to reduce carbon imprints. Clean energy is a must for survival of the globe.

Humans are done with oil. It is written in the sky in carbon.

The era of oil is over.

One era to another. We have to be on the move.

The Gulf Widens...

Rest of Asia In Doldrums. South- East Asia Revving.

Other than Trump finally we have some real piece of good news. Ha Ha!

Feb 2016

News: Has Japan's grand attempt to reflate the world's third largest economy failed? The Bank of Japan (BOJ) crossed over into uncharted territory, pushing interest rates below zero for the first time ever.

For the first time ever.

In just two days in Feb-2016 the Japanese stock market was down nearly 8%. The GDP figures indicated that the Japanese economy was shrinking again.

There is a strange problem in Japan where large corporations are sitting of piles of cash - as much as 3 trillion. But are not spending it. Because they are afraid their investment will not get returns in the current and the foreseeable future. The Japan businessmen know for sure the economy is on a major downswing.

Hold on to dear money!

Exports in Asian giants Japan, China and South Korea drop by double digits.

Toshiba, the television to nuclear reactor Japanese conglomerate woke up one fine day to find it had losses amounting to billions of dollars. By early 2017 it was clear Toshiba nuclear (US) faced bankruptcy and its employees an uncertain future.

But the really good news is that the other part of Asia is humming with positive energy. The people here sense the momentum and are excited.

The South East Asia.

It seems like the gravity is shifting from the West to the East. And there's only real good news here.

Feb-2017: ISRO launches 104 satellites in one rocket. This is a world record. That is an Indian space agency.

South East Asia Revving.

CYCLES PREDICT A CRASH

Corporates need to forecast downward graphs. We can't keep going up all the time. The economy moves in cycles. Study of the cyclical trends of modern economic history should be the baseline for every management executive. The reasons for the ebb and flow of modern economy has to be analyzed and the rise and fall has to be factored in. The cyclical trends are a powerful means of prediction and knowing the events likely to happen will put decision making back in human hands rather than let us be overwhelmed by random events that coalesce to form a tsunami.

The discoverer of the K waves was executed because he predicted the end of certain type of civilization decades before it actually fell apart — communism.

The K waves. The K waves reportedly predict a downswing in 2017. Other cycles of economy for instance the 8.6 year cycle (the last recession was in 2008) converge to the same year. Cyclical theories too coalesce to the year 2017. And that is unnerving.

During the great depression of 1929 people lost homes, the rich became poor, millions had to stand in soup lines just to survive.

During the stock market crash of 1987 23% value was lost in a single day.

The point is, bad things do happen. From time to time. In fact, till date there have been 33 recessions since the start of capitalism. There has been no expansion more than 10 years in the entire history of capitalism. The longest expansion started in 1991 and ended in the dot com bust. The second longest started in 1961 and lasted nearly 9 years. Currently we are in the third longest expansion running more than 8 years of unbridled euphoria. And now even without any kind of cycle prediction we need to accept that there may be a 'times up' in the horizon.

As of Nov 2016, 19 of the 28 European countries are in huge debt. 30 banks in Europe have stocks that are trading at historic lows. These include the global big banks like Societe Generale, Paribas and Santander.

Japan's debt is 2.5 times its GDP. And worse, nobody in Japan is investing knowing that they may not get their money back.

Negative interest rates in some countries. You have to pay the bank to keep your money.

The debt pile of the US government keeps growing. It will cross $20 trillion and that will be a milestone of sorts. Just a couple of months after the Trump inauguration. And Trump plans to up the spend. What happens to the debt?

Once Euro and Japan crash, the wealthy there will try to shift their money to USA. The stocks will rise. But only just. It's panic money. The USA too will not be able to sustain the huge influx because the fundamentals will not support. And the markets will crash. First, a rise in US stocks followed by a mighty fall. This is one of the scenarios how it might play out.

The great depression of 2017. Big banks will collapse like ninepins. Stock markets across the globe will swing down faster than you can react, bonds too. The most valued investment across the world, will go up in smoke. Likely in the last quarter of 2017. Because by then the world would know the Trump effects.

Don't panic. It is not a prediction. Just a likely scenario. But note 'likely'. There are other ways it could happen.

By the end of 2016 Warren Buffet has a rumored 55 billion dollars in cash. That is the most 'rumored' cash he has in 40 years. Why has he not invested in the market?

By the end of 2016 George Soros has increased his short position 5 times.

Several times in 2016 Jim Rogers says he is staying away from the US stock market.

These are the 3 legends of investing this century. They don't seem to have much confidence in the US stock market.

It's about time too. From 2009, 8 years of bull market (Much of it though is by way of dubious 'easy' money). Now there is going to be a reversal-interest rate increases and the Dow has factored in all the good news. You need to beat the good news to keep the Dow going up.

The worry that the flood of cash has encouraged needless risky financial decisions is real. And the result of this easy money on other economies is an illusion.

Illusion of cash. Illusion of investment. Illusion of economy.

We have created an illusionary global economy. The real economy is uncomfortable with illusions. Its basic nature is to get back to reality. Sooner or later.

Between 2017-2020 as the economy attempts to get back to reality will there be a crash at some point of time ? Maybe in the last quarter of 2017 — when the world gets to see the effects of the Trump decisions?

Because the primary mover of Dow today is Trump. If Trump wins the Dow wins. If Trump loses...

2017 - 2020: The Coming Crash?

THE RESULT

The results can be read in the preparation. What you will be is in exponential proportion to what you do now.

You can judge the action by the result. And the result by the action.

Glance at the 2016 results. What horrendous decisions over the last decade has led to these results?

Venezuela: 720 % inflation

Greece: Debt Crisis

Italy: A banking cesspool

China debt to GDP: 300%

USA: QE Bubble and $ 20 Trillion Debt

Japan: Negative interest rates

Saudis: Lenders turn borrowers

In 2016 Latin America contracted 0.7% due to the effect of lower commodity prices and capital flight as the commodity super boost came to an end. There was recession in the big Latino countries - Brazil, Argentina and Venezuela.

Brazil is largest of the Latin American countries and is the 5th largest in the world in terms of purchasing power parity (PPP) – goes to show that the top economies in the world are all affected.

Here is the link for more on Latin Americana.

http://www.focus-economics.com/regions/latin-america

37. The breadth of bad economic news spans the globe. From one end to another. With only a few islands of relief. These will also get dragged into the connected quagmire.

The stark landscape of history is a pointer to this immutable law. The indications are precursors of the results. From Goliath who fell to Lehmann bros which vanished. The indicators do tell a story. If we only listen and understand.

Deutsche bank is much bigger than Lehmann Bros whose collapse led to the 2008 recession.

Warren Buffet calls Derivatives 'Weapons of Mass Destruction'. They are known to be extremely toxic and can bring down banks like nothing else. And Deutsche has $46 trillion of these. The illiquid asset is $10 billion. Worse, the actual value of its assets is a mystery. It may be much below its shown book value. Deutsche bank put its subsidiary on the block. But nobody is willing to buy a Deutsche subsidiary.

An Italian court has slapped charges on Deutsche Bank over its role in covering up and falsifying Italy's oldest bank Monte Paschi losses and mistrades. The USA DOJ has slapped $ 14 billion fine and settled for around $ 7 billion.

More than all these Deutsche bank is heavily networked with several prominent banks. If it goes down it will take a few others too alongwith it. The stock price of Deutsche is below its 2008 recession price. And the grand top-up is that Deutsche bank is struggling to earn profit.

This time, will Deutsche bank will be the first of the big banks to collapse. And others will follow?

One third of Eurozone bad debts are in Italy. Portugal is in the dumps, Greece faces another deadline in July, Spain unemployment is bad, France makes news with Marine Le Pen and Frexit. The Stoxx chart shows a Shoulder-Head-Shoulder pattern in 2017 that is 40% off its record high it saw way back in 2000. Continuation of this pattern will take the Stoxx to a new low. There seem to be no redeeming factors. The global fall might start with Eurozone after all, while much of the focus is on USA.

In 2008 it was the recession. This time will it be the depression? A stitch in time saves nine. The time has passed. Will the nine bad banks survive 2017?

The warning is in the signs and the results. Either we take it or we don't.

SPECULATION

Speculation is the opposite of utility. If you gain 100 today, you might as well lose 1000 tomorrow. There is no logic to speculation. Event based decisions are not speculations.

There is a mythic story of a dice game between two rival kings vying for the same kingdom. As the game of dice progresses the innocent and good king overwhelmed by the game keeps upping the stake until he pledges his kingdom. And he loses the throw of the dice and his kingdom!

Speculation since historical times has been bringing down men, families, populations and kingdoms.

Will the speculative trades on the back of easy money or the big banks speculative coverage including derivatives contribute to bring down the global order of economy in 2017?

All it takes is a couple of big reversals and the speculative positions will fall with a domino effect. A pack of cards.

The throw of dice has already been done.

Nobody has ever won a kingdom by speculation. Since mythic times.

Derivatives the complex financial bets were captured into an equation − the Black Scholes Equation that was later awarded the Nobel prize. The Black-Scholes equation was like a roadmap for derivative trades and traders got onto it expanding the derivative market massively. The derivative market before the 2008 crash reached one quadrillion dollars per year! The traders forgot the pre-condition of the equation − the equation was for a certain market condition. If the market condition changed... The market condition changed. The world's 'best' big banks which blindly followed the equation like a donkey (not pricing in the changed market condition) collapsed.

Derivatives are speculative. Derivatives become official casinos when common sense is lost (like it happened in 2008 – when the market conditions changes traders didn't change the formula and the ended in creating chaos). Derivatives are now 7 times the size of global economy.

INVESTMENT STRATEGY: 2017 – 2020

Recession – Normal – Supernormal.

This will decide the investment strategy.

In the second half of 2017 gold may touch 700 dollars. Someone predicted this towards end of 2016 and I couldn't make sense of it. But in Dec-2016 when Fed increased the interest rate by 0.25% gold fell. With two more increases (at the minimum) it is now easy to understand the possibility that gold may touch the downside. On the other hand the prediction that the upper range is 1350 and even 2000 also makes sense. With Eurozone cracking, Japan heading towards deflation and USA reeling under QE and increasing debtpile, gold just shooting through the roof seems plausible. The Trump acceptance speech changed the entire perception built around him throughout the campaign and in turn turned the globe topsy-turvy. The stocks were expected to crash but went up instead. And gold went down.

In Dec 2016 Trump 'mania' made gold go down and in Jan 2017 Trump 'fear factor' is making gold go up. In Mar-2017 the Fed interest rate hike is making gold go down again. Subsequently there is a fast recovery-up again

This just goes to show we are living in highly unpredictable times.

Then how do we invest?

Strong dollar: A strong dollar is bad for emerging markets. If rest of the globe is weak can the US do a bumper business? Will not other countries try to do business with countries other than USA since they will be more cost attractive.

A strong dollar may therefore be its own negative pole. And so the rise in dollar will have a cap due its implications.

Companies outsourced to cut costs. If they bring back business to USA will they manage to remain cost competitive since the cost of doing business in the USA will be much more than that of doing the same in the outsourced country?

4IR: We have been through the internet.com - digital android – internet ecomm wave. Isn't there a possibility that the Data-Analytics-AI-Robotics-Drone wave may just turbo charge propel us into another decade of economic wellbeing. A wave has ripple effect and with other positives can again make all dire predictions topsy-turvy. Could we have a Data-Analytics-AI-Robotics-Drone driven 4IR (4th Industrial Revolution) that can rescue us after a recession.

So there is a pull and a push, a positive and a negative a north and a south pole to the global economy. It has always been that historically. Periods of economic superlatives interspersed with transition and downright recession-depression. We are now trundling along. We are in a period of transition. Neither here nor there.

We are living with memories of a not so far prosperous decade hoping for another. During 2017-2020 whether the globe buckles and collapses or trundles along or is pulled up is unpredictable.

How at all do we read the situation and how do we invest?

Do we invest for a recession, normal times or super normal times?

So here is the solution that I have for you that no matter whether a recession, a normal or a super normal future it makes you a winner. It has some ideas you may not even have thought about. Some ideas you will pass along but which will remain with you and as you carry on and as you see events happening around you these same ideas will begin to make sense to you. And some ideas you will instantly recognize as your own.

So here we go. The approach to Invest and Win. No matter what.

THE INVESTMENT

I suggest a 10-20 % allocation in each of these categories.

1. Metals: Lithium, Cobalt and Graphene. Invest and Hold.

Lithium. It is not only used in electric cars but some US states have started using Lithium batteries as electric stores for peak usage. Facilities made of lithium batteries. Added to the lithium in the electric cars. Expect a demand peak every year. Cobalt is also an electric metal.

Graphene. It will be all over the place in the coming future. Get into graphene early. Jim Rogers already owns it. It is always the early birds that get the meat. For more on this wonder crystal and futuristic scenarios read Top 100 Technology Trends (By Piam).

2. Dow Jones (USA)

2017: Highly Volatile.

Best Strategy: Get Out Early 2017. Sell on the Highs of the Tax Break News. And then Stay Away.

Next Strategy: Wait and watch till at least 2 Fed rate increases.

Risk: High Risk after mid March-2017.

48 Once we reach the point when Trump announces the tax breaks from then on the risk-return on US stocks will be highly skewed. If the Fed increases interest rates twice or more then it is a compounded risk. If Trump does not announce the tax breaks and instead is focused on healthcare then too get out of the US stocks. Early 2017 would be the best time to sell US stocks and wait and watch in the sidelines.

If you still want to invest:

Then do so when the Dow dips. Actually it would be a good idea to wait until Fed hikes interest rates twice. Wait, watch how the Dow reacts and then take action.

When you invest you need to be highly stock specific. Your stock selection has to be just right.

Be very informed – business news, stock specific news, Be very quick and Be very grounded if you are investing in US stocks in the year 2017.

If you have reached a target price and have achieved a profit it will be better if you sell on every rise.

You can also split into Trading and Investment in the Dow Jones. Trading can be quite stressful and you can do it only if you know about stocks. The intention is to reduce the holding price. But it is tough and is only for those who have keen insight and real time involvement.

With US stocks in 2017 the action should be – Book Profit.

Alphabet: Flush with cash as much as 85 billion dollars, with strong positioning in AI and AI products and continuing growth in legacy income. The past current and future are all overweight.

It's committed. America will see $ 1 Trillion inflows into infrastructure. Get into infra and energy stocks (before they fly off the handle).

IOT: Cars talking to each other, remote control houses and healthcare device are just the tip of IOT (internet of things). IOT will increase mobile - data traffic. It's a buy for data REITS, chip stock and network stocks. As a billionaire said "Data is the new oil." Same applies to analytics. So have a presence in this space.

Data, analytics and new technology.

Remember there is a stock high and low in each year and there is a substantial gap between the high and the low. And the Dow Jones has already built in that Trump will deliver. What if he doesn't?

Gold stocks as a hedge. Be selective. Actually gold stocks seem to be a good idea if you get one at the right price.

Finally, here is the link for top stocks in USA for 2017 from Barrons.

Top 10 USA Stocks 2017. After you open the link you may need to log in to get the full story.

http://www.barrons.com/articles/top-10-stock-picks-for-2017-1480748688

This is an indicative link. There are many more stocks you could and should consider.

Dow is at an all-time high and has factored in all the good news. Not even bad news but just absence of good news will take Dow down in 2017. The time to book profits is fast approaching − the time when the US stocks will soar the most in 2017 - when Trump will announce his tax breaks or the markets realize that Trump will not announce tax breaks in 2017− Just Get Out No Matter What. Get out in mid Mar-2017.

Tips N Trades

Hold those stocks which you are sure of.

When you are unsure and you are in the positive, sell instinctively.

When a stock goes up excessive to its normal range of PE and can't be explained - Sell.

There are always stocks that are available at reasonable or buyable PE's (in case a stock has slipped past your grasping hands).

Every stock has a year high and a low — you get what I mean? So knowing when to sell and when to buy is key to success.

Buy and Sell with a certain insight and news based. Because Trump is on the scene, you have to adjust your perspective to the policies that will be unleashed and their impact. For instance, about pharma he said 'pharma companies make a killing with their drug prices being so high.' Which could be a fact.

So either skip or be reactive (instant decisions and reactions to news) with pharma until the implications are clear.

Keep watching for signs of recession. In case you feel the jitters check out the 17 point Survival Guide (in this very book).

For USA Buy only if you must; know your stock (company) well — at the time you buy it, at the time you hold it and at the time you sell it; Sell on Instinct (especially if you are even or have a profit); be informed every single day (either stock news channels, online or alerts) and know that there is going to be a year high and a year low.

Again we reiterate: The Dow keeps breaking records. And the best time to book profits is fast approaching - And that is when Trump announces the tax breaks. If it meets expectations Dow will soar. That will be the best time in a long time the best time to book profits. And get away. From then on it will be performance and not hope that will guide the Dow.

And we all know hope and optimism is one thing and performing and living up to expectations something else altogether. And if Trump backtracks and doesn't announce the tax break then markets will have a breakdown. They are at a stretched high already. Mid Mar 2017 will be the best time to sell US stocks. You may not get to see Dow at that level again in 2017.

3. Emerging Markets: Emerging markets have historically returned much better returns than developed countries. The World Bank forecasts 6.7% growth in 2017 and much higher in the coming years for this country. This will be shining star of the financial world between 2017-2020.

India.

By the next 2 decades the purchasing power of India will overtake that of America.

And you want to be there to see it happen.

Here are some of the companies that will be at the forefront of the India growth story. And many of them are spreading their wings across the globe. If you want to live the American dream all over again go to India. It is happening there. We strongly suggest more allocation to this geography.

Here are some of the companies that will be at the forefront of the India growth story. And many of them are spreading across the globe. We have also given the CMP (current market price at the time we are recommending them).

1. Apollo Hospitals: An established chain of reputed hospitals, multi-country operations, health insurance and medical colleges. It aims to train 100000 students per year by 2020.CMP: Rs.1200

2. Heromotor Corp: India is the 2nd largest populous country in the world. And Heromotor is one of the best known motorcycle and 2 wheeler manufacturers. India's population and consumption is growing. Need we say more?

Heromotor Corp not only has overseas targets but multicountry manufacturing hubs. More motorcycles in more countries. The next auto giant will be from India. Bye Bye Japan. CMP: Rs.3020

3. Spice Jet: This has placed a multibillion order to purchase a couple of hundred planes. If oil does not go up you can get 100-300% appreciation from current price in this stock. CMP Rs.65

4. Apollo Tyres: When auto is on a roll tyres should be rolling along! Autos roll on tyres! CMP: Rs. 185.

5. Mahanagar Gas: Gas distribution to Mumbai city. Introduced gas run scooters. CMP: Rs.850.

6. Aashiana Housing: Affordable housing is the current hot spot. Aashiana Housing was ranked by Forbes amongst 'Asia's Best Under a Billion Companies'. CMP: Rs.175

7. Escorts: Farm machinery, city equipment and tractors. It is on a technology upheaval and multi country export mission. CMP: Rs.465

8. Kotak Bank: A premier private sector bank. What's a portfolio without a private bank in a take off economy. CMP Rs.775

9. Dwarikesh Sugar: India is a sweet country. It is a country of festivals. Sugar your holdings. CMP: Rs.390

10. Havell's Electricals. Every house needs them. And affordable housing is the theme. Havell's has taken over the consumer biz of its competitor and planned a big foray into consumer durables. CMP: Rs.410

11. GAIL: Gas transporter with stake in gas distribution. CMP: Rs.360

12. Biocon: Pharma and biotech leader with multicountry operations. In partnership with Mylan has 2 biosimilar (biologic similar) drugs. Has had positive FDA responses. A powerstock. CMP: 1070

13. Amar Raja Batteries: Top end auto batteries. New and replacement. Consistently great stock. CMP: Rs. 850

14. ITC : The leader in FMCG. CMP: Rs.280.

Bata: Shoes. Why leave them out. The mark of a man. And a woman! Bata is adding Hush Puppies to its products in 2017. A lot of significant sideway movement every now and then. Buy and Sell. Buy and Sell. Buy and Sell. This one is for the traders. CMP: Rs.450

Reliance Industries: The Big Boss of Indian Stocks. Oil and gas. And now telecom. Trailblazing mobile telephony it has garnered 100 million users in just months. It has started monetizing the 100 million users. Hmm. CMP: Rs.1200

REC: Electricity distribution. Benefits from price increase of electricity this month. CMP: RS 170

D-Mart: 100% profits on listing. Ace Investor created this supermarket chain. Imagine owing Wal-Mart on a growth curve. You missed Wal-Mart. Don't ever miss this. CAGR of upto 50%. CMP: 570

Fiem Industries: Auto Components to the Who's Who of Auto companies. Multibagger stock. CMP: RS 880

As of Feb 2017 the Indian stocks are surging up. Their Finance Minister has unleashed a growth beast. Be in India more than anywhere else between 2017-2020. The World Bank agrees.

Indian Multibaggers: An Indicative List with RMP (Recommended Market Price). Some of the stocks listed below have given above 1000% returns.

1. Coromandel Fertilizer: Fertilizers.
RMP: Rs. 310

2. Jubilant Life: Pharmaceutical and life sciences
RMP: Rs 700

3. Dewan Housing Finance: Housing Finance
RMP: Rs 310

4. Hatsun Agro Food: FMCG Food
RMP: 490

5. Repco Home Finance: 20% growth projected
RMP: Rs 650

6. Ramco Cement: Realty Cement

RMP: Rs. 650

7. Jayant Agro : Agri based company. Super stock.

RMP: Rs.670

8. Century Ply: Household

RMP: Rs 230

9. Caplin Point Lab: Pharma. The stock that rose 11,800% in a few years. Expected CAGR above 25 %. Entering USA in 2017-2018. RMP: Rs 376

10. IG Petro: Third largest specialty chemicals used in construction and paints. RMP: Rs 320

11. Dredging Corp: Government Stake Sale

RMP: Rs 460

12. GIC: Government Stake Sale Proposed

RMP Rs 295

(BEML and BEL are some of the other companies in which government stake sale is proposed.)

The above are well researched stocks, well entrenched in the core of the Indian economy. Please check the yearly high – low, PE, EPS and other parameters at the time of investing to maximize your gains.

Emerging Markets: South East Asia

I would recommend more allocation to South East Asian markets. They have factored in all the bad news (while Dow has factored in all the good news). Check with your financial advisor for other emerging market opportunities.

Again it will be 3 types : Trading, Investing and a Mix of trading and investing. It depends on what you consider best for you.

Emerging markets will provide buying opportunities in 2017. Due to weak global factors.

4. Oil: Oil will likely trade between 40 to 55 dollars in 2017. This could be the safe zone for an oil trader. Shale will find it unattractive at the lower range and will rake it in above 55. OPEC or no OPEC shale production in USA has a say in the oil price.

5. AI, Drones, Robotics: Be in this space for exponential growth. Flying drone taxis in Dubai, robotics in surgery, artificial intelligence everywhere. Take a step forward. Be in the future before future overtakes you.

6. Dividend Paying Stocks: If you get them at low enough price. Do the maths with your financial advisor.

7. Agri: The perfect hedge against a downturn. Because food will always be needed. But going beyond that.agri is an entire industry in itself. Exploring it, if it interests you can be rewarding and it can be an effective hedge if times get tough. A bit of connection with agri seems just right considering the times we live in.

8. Overseas : It can be overseas. Why not? I know for many of you this might be a new idea. But then the times are topsy - turvy.

Real Estate in India: Trump has Trump towers coming up in India. No wonder he is so savvy a businessman. He saw the potential much earlier. Real estate in the fastest growing major economy in the world. It's a no brainer.

It can give a regular rental as well as a capital appreciation. Check with your financial advisor about other emerging countries real estate opportunities.

Farmland also can give you a fixed monthly, quarterly or yearly income. How about owning an exotic mango or pomegranate and other tropical fruit farm. Sounds juicy.

9. Solar and Wind: Firstsolar (USA), Sunpower (USA) are leaders in solar. Elon Musk has an integrated solar roof with Solarcity. It is not the thing on the roof. It is the roof! So there. When the man planning voyage to Mars is into solar. Be in solar and wind.

Miscellaneous.

Trading: Check the 1 year high and low. Every year there will a high and a low. Useful for buying and selling. Also keep a watch on your favorite stocks. The nature of the market is to go up and down. Many times you will see your stocks at your target low and high prices.

Treasury bonds, mortgage backed securities not issued by the government and US bank bonds. Check with your financial advisor for details.

Gold and Silver: Buy around fed rate hikes for low prices. Accumulate on dips every quarter.

The Motley Fool: Last but surely not the least! He has a track record of beating the experts!

Now that we have a strategy. Let's test it.

Objective: Since we cannot predict the future course of the next 2-3 years we have designed an investment that can take care of normal or supernormal times or a recession.

What have we done:

1. Advised Lithium, Cobalt and Graphene as the new age safe metals.

2. Keep gold and silver but invest in Lithium and Graphene.

3. Advised agri as a hedge against a downturn. Includes overseas farmland (A novel idea).

4. Advised overseas real estate investment. Some regions are better off than others. Some are in a growth curve. Some are aged economies. Invest in young and growing economies they will take you along (A novel advise).

5. Advised 3 types of holding in the stocks (Trading, Investing and a Mix of both). Will ensure lowering of cost of stock holdings.

6. Advised action around Fed rate increases.

7. Presence in new energy: solar particularly.

8. Presence in recession proof (shock absorber) stocks such as Alphabet and technology stocks. Because no recession can stop the march of time and the advance of technology!

Test

Normal and Supernormal: If times are normal there is no doubt the above investment will enjoy super profits. Other than the US stocks we have invested everything as normal. Which is good. It is in fact very good not to be in US stocks post Mar-2017.

Recession: In a recession the main focus is to survive the current situation. In case of recession while certain emerging market stocks can take a hit the hedge against a downturn agri (national or overseas) will maintain us during that time and the technology stocks will ensure our future. In addition we will have dividend paying stocks and bonds.

If you manage to sell the stocks at a right time (Mar 2017 in USA) you will be those among the richer and well off population in case of a downswing or even a recession down the line. The agri will be working for you and the new technology will be taking care of your future. If you had been trading, even if you have stocks the price would have been lowered.

So, in a recession there is a multi-pronged approach that will sustain and also ensure a superb future.

With this strategy, in normal and supernormal times you will have many sources of income. In a recession you will have a stable and dependable platform and a bright and supra-profitable future.

Whatever the situation, this Piam Investment Strategy (2017-2020) is positioned to ride the new technology and South East Asian emerging market wave that is just on the anvil. As a hedge for recession this strategy will ensure you are stable.

This strategy has a slew of options that you can pick and choose as you consider suitable for you and your family.

Keep Silver and Invest in Lithium. You get the drift? While we have the traditional stuff we are invested and in fact positioned towards the future.

How to trade in gold and silver. The gold dilemma of 2017. Will it go up or will it go down? Check out the gold section in the 16 point Recession Survival Guide. And take a decision. We find it unpredictable in the short term. Fed rate hike tends to lower gold-silver prices. There are 2-3 Fed hikes possible this year. We recommend a trading strategy in the short term and keep adding a bit around every fed rate hike to get the best low prices.

Keep 10% as an investment in gold and silver. News Based Trade (Buy on dips and Sell on highs). Maybe silver with its industrial uses may just bridge the gold - silver gap and may perform better.

If you are not actively trading and only want to invest then there are both negative and positive pulls to gold and silver and you need to have a long term hold. Gold and silver could go down (fed rate hikes) as much as up (Trump policy fear and global politico-economic weakness) in the short term.

You can also check out our Gold-Silver Fed Trading Strategy and Gold-Silver Offensive Defensive Strategy.

The Gold-Silver Defensive-Offensive Strategy

To maximize the profit and also keep it as a safe haven. (Allocate a portion for 5 year holding, allocate a portion for trading) Trade around news like Fed interest changes and for long term we find gold will make a splash especially if you buy at around the Fed rate hike low prices.

The Gold-Silver Fed Trading Strategy.

The Fed plans to increase the interest rate 3 times in 2017. And the 100% certain way to invest or trade in gold and silver is the weeks before and the weeks after the rate decision.

If the unemployment is below 5% and stable or improving, the industrial production is stable or increasing then a rate hike is certain.

Short Gold or SELL Gold a couple of weeks prior to the Fed meet that has intent to increase interest rate (not all fed meets raise interest rates). Immediately after fed announces the hike or 1 – 3 days after the fed hike (depends on how the market views the rate hike and whether gold is recovering quickly) BUY Gold. You have just made a HUGE profit.

Do it every time Fed meets with intent to hike rate in 2017. But read the indicators carefully: the unemployment rate and the industrial production index (already described). And the Fed intent to hike rate as indicated by comments of the Fed members in the run up to their meet.

Same for silver. You can go twinning.

TRUMP VERSUS THE GLOBAL FORCES

Trump is seeming more and more sensible with each passing day (though the insensible part still remains it seems to be progressively muted).

Trump and Russia. Russia becoming a friend of America (the most shocking thing ever!) may not be such a bad idea - considering China! And who else but Trump might have been the only President ever to make Russia a 'friend' of America. So predictions of any kind go out of the window. I would rather have a strategy than a prediction. Because the world is going topsy-turvy.

Trump and China. The boundaries are being sharply etched. The voices grow shrill. We thought the big bad banks of Europe may lead to an economic crash and we have a situation building up — in South China Sea. China is aggressive and has claimed and built structures on the islands possibly stuffing them with the latest ammunition.

Trump and the Ban. It turns out though that one in every two Americans apparently endorse the ban and it is one of Trump's popular decisions in the USA just after taking over. Nobody wants radical terrorism and he has a strong stand over that.

The ban on certain countries. Could there have been better ways to do it, more discreet a soft glove approach so that the radicals are isolated rather than a community being polarized?

He has ticked off Russia over Crimea. He went after China the whole of Dec-2016 and Jan-2017. In Feb 2017 China tested a missile that could carry 10 nuclear war heads. But then later he called China and stated USA respected 'One China Policy'. He has also modified the ban to a merit based protocol that some countries are already following making it seem harmless.

He seems to know how far to go and when to withdraw.

Could you have imagined Hillary taking some of the tough steps that he has? He can take the bull by the horns. Hillary might have hee-hawed with much to be found in ill concealed emails. Maybe what happens, happens for the good. With Hillary, Russia would have been an arch enemy and China would have made a killing in the US market.

The oil affluence of Russia was all out there at Davos 2017. The Russians are already gung ho about America doing business in Russia. What was all the hullabaloo about anyways? USA - Russia cold war. Some global hallucination of the history bin.

Is Russia conniving and 'evil'? Some may ask 'As much as USA has been?' Has not USA funded terror states until it hit home? Did it have to take a home strike to awake it? A global leader who was not averse to think about itself in the garb of strategy and tactics. And now we have a straight talking guy who just gets to the core of the matter.

Why carry decade old debris. Move over. The new has arrived. The screen saver of history has changed.

Fool and genius, the one is mistaken for the other. Often. (This is just an exaggeration, a figure of speech to put things in a perspective). Is that the case with Trump? Who else could have made it possible even to imagine for a moment Americans doing business and investing in Russia. But that was the flavor of the evening at Davos 2017.

Van Gogh sold 1 painting in his entire life. Post his death he was recognized as a genius. Bill Gates says Trump has a chance to be a Kennedy. If Trump manages, he could indeed be a Kennedy. Because he has inherited a tough and unpredictable future. Geopolitically tough and economically unpredictable. Which means people are ready to celebrate with him, inspite of all that has happened, if he pulls it off. That is a big IF and not as smooth as cheese as the Dow makes it seem.

You have to give it to the man. He has insight, he is open, he knows how far he can go (that is the defining border between insight and insanity!) and he can move ahead amidst severe criticism.

If South China Sea is simmering, North Korea is launching recognizable missiles as well unspecified projectiles. In response USA has started deploying Terminal High Altitude Area Defense (THAAD) system in the Korean region. China and Russia have already voiced their strong opposition. North Korean missiles drop in Japanese seas and North Korea uses the word 'war' like we eat breakfast. Picture the ban against this backdrop. You see more opposing forces.

Will Trump be able to contain these forces or will he allow these to become major flashpoints to add a political dimension to the economic weakness in the Euro – Japan - USA axis.

THE HI-BYE TRUMP EFFECT

He may be loud, rude, offensive, brutish and uncouth. But there is sound logic in many of his decisions and he acts in the prime interest of USA. At the core he has good intentions for USA. No doubt.

He has reined in federal employees pay packages and stopped excess staff intake. He twitters policy - Airforce to cut cost, healthcare and drug price high. Are not pharma companies making polevaulting profits? Every day is an action day. There is no doubt he acts in America's interests.

American engineers' society has rated America's infrastructure at 'D'. If your report card showed a D you knew where you stood. USA dams, spillovers, road bridges need an urgent makeover. Many are decades old. Trump's $ 1 trillion in this segment is not only an economic push that will have spillover effect but is the need of the hour for America's infrastructure.

He has his priorities right : I am _ POTUS.

Open all over twitter, no cloak and dagger. No Nixon stuff.

But then what's the issue?

He shouted at the prime minister of an ally country and banged the phone on him probably. That's probably not how you would want to deal with heads of state. He mimics a disabled reporter.

He wants a wall across two countries (but again his intent is pro-USA!) funded by taxes.

He rides roughshod. It's the way he goes about it at times. Not all things should be in the face — take it or leave it.

Trump proposes, the opposition cuts it into several pieces and what ends up is not particularly what you would want.

Between Trump, the fed and the senate will the US economy get what it deserves?

I am highly skeptical.

HI - Bye.

Yes. If Trump delivers it's a Hi. If he doesn't it's a Bye. Not for him alone but for everything much of USA aspires for.

THE WORLD IN A SNAPSHOT

Fitch Rating: India grows at 7.1% and maintains high growth rate from 2017-2020. Be in India.

USA : Uncertain. Will Trump be able to pull it off ?

Eurozone: France has an anti-Eurozone as a leading candidate — Marine Le Pen.

Japan : Limp.

South American: Deep weakness

Middle East: Transition from oil.

Trump praised Ford for reinvesting in the USA. As more and more companies reinvest in USA unemployment figures will go down and industrial production index will go up. This will just make the Fed increase interest rate rightaway. But then cost to the companies will increase. The H1B visa decision will also increase the cost of resources and talent may go to other welcoming regions.

Added to this, a stronger dollar and tariffs on the anvil may make trade to flow to other countries that may offer lower prices. Dow is already at an all time high. The Fed has indicated 3 rate hikes. Considering all these the Dow is likely to offer buying opportunities in late 2017. Wait for big dips in the Dow to buy in the USA.

Cash: Keep cash. Cash is king. And queen. But ensure to keep in those banks that will be up and running in tough times. Again consider having accounts in multiple banks.

Emerging Markets: Every time fed hikes rate there is a stronger dollar and a weaker emerging market as of now. Time your buys to the market dips in emerging markets that happen preceding or just after the fed hikes. Have exposure to emerging markets. You can do a Buy on dips and Sell on Rise approach.

Hold long term. Yes you can also hold long term if you are investing company and sector specific. And you bought at the bottom. Well known emerging markets investment guru Mark Mobius of Templeton Funds (emerging market focused fund) prefers China ahead of India in the long term. Yes, 2017 will see emerging markets take a dip. Particularly the days around the Fed interest rate increases. LIC, the largest equity investor in India just cut its equity exposure by 20%. The stronger dollar will push down the emerging markets offering you the opportunity to get some of the best companies at low prices. Remember the owner of the Jaguar cars is an Indian company. And they are well on the way to touch 1 million cars in sales by 2020. There are such gems in India which is currently the fastest growing major global economy. From designer fashionables to software to automobile and pharma-biotech and infra engineering you can get some of the best companies to invest.

Consider Indonesia, S.Korea, Taiwan and other emerging South Asian countries. South Korea and Taiwan are in the focus of foreign funds.

Get in touch with your financial advisor. Have an in-depth discussion. You get the information you want. You take the decision you want.

India is the best. Their only problem is the huge bad debts (NPA) in their banking sector (which have had a refinance). And it is in the finest hands at the moment.

The Indian stockmarket is expected to increase by 6 % - 18% in 2017. The last quarter of 2017 I would stay away from stocks – globally. Dredging Corp rose 15 % in a single day as news filtered that the Indian government is divesting stake. Other companies that the government is considering stake sale are BEML, BEL and GIC. Stake sale is a huge price driver and you can get into these shares.

Follow names. Elon Musk, Buffet, Jeff Bezos. Check out what they are doing. These and other trailblazers. There are several small companies that will just blast their way into the world and make space for themselves.

Subscribe or just be in touch news, online, social media, twitter whatever.

By 2020 we have 3 years in which to digest or be able to read the implications of QE stop, China excess and Oil price fall and the Euro Exit and Euro potential Exits.

TECH SWING

Tech change can swing it.

Automation can take away jobs. That's the ask from the CEO. Else why would they opt to automate? Corporates will want to hack jobs. Save costs, improve precision. On the other side it means tech has gained so much capability that it can take over. The age of tech.

Automation will reach levels of analysis. The repetitive data recognition and data entry ask is primitive. Analytical automatons is the expectation. And we already have systems that help diagnose cancers as well as treat. Seated next to a specialist human doctor will be a specialist automaton doctor.

New Technology Breakthrough: New tech is what will change the entire diaspora. It has the power to change the world on its own. Wherever and whatever you can — Be. Not only invest but be part of new technology. You can be not just an investor, you can be a techie or a technopreneur.

New Age Hunt: Hunt for these and different ways to invest in them. This need not be only by way of stocks. Invest your career. Marissa Meyer invested her career in Google as a fresher. Today she is the CEO of Yahoo. AI, robotics, self driven gadgets, smart applications, digital wears.

New Age Metals: Lithium, Cobalt and Graphene. Same story here. Invest in these in any way you can. Right from the companies that mine them to the companies that use them.

AI and robotics are evolving fast, under the radar. Amazon delivers by drones - the logistic guys don't have a job; Budweiser delivers beer with self driven trucks - out go the drivers; chatbots talk products - customer care and sales girls nyet; Exit formalities in companies, accounts and finance all the way upto disease diagnosis managed by AI - cut down on experts here. Robots. They will be all over the place from elderly care and surgery to entertainment and being your best buddy. So it's a combined thrust of old age cranking economy and the new age transition that will present a striking real time change that you will have to manage.

It's not only investing money but investing yourself that can make the difference between survival and riding the crest of the gigantic waves of witnessed historical time transition.

2020 - A wave. Flying cars, self driving cars, hyperloop, IOT and global cloud, drones, chatbots, AI, robotics – robot friend, robot butler, robot medic, root surgeon, robot singer, robot actor, robot, robot, robot.

Surf the technology wave.

RECORD OR RECESSION

What about the current? Times are unpredictable and so is Trump. If the economy ticks due to Trump, the OPEC decisions, China tightening policies and the emerging Asian countries; then instead of a recession we may pass by with even a good economy. So much the better for all of us.

But on the other hand if things do not hold together then we have crisis that can be mild, moderate or severe. This seems likely too. Read the 16 point 'Survival Guide', monitor the situation, stay connected and apply the survival tips. Timing is crucial. Exit is as important as entry.

The longest time we have been without a recession is 10 years - In the entire history of capitalism. Now we have completed 8 years. In 2 years either we break the record or we have a recession. I have given you enough information in this book for you to decide. And to act.

CEO'S RAKE IT IN

Even thieves have ethics. What about businessmen and bankers?

Some executives are known to take hundreds of millions of dollars in bonuses. Executives live the high life and we know some buy islands to frolic around. I have nil against that provided it is all well-earned (and not by insider trading). And shared.

Volkswagen company faced a crisis over its rigging of emission tests. There was widespread disbelief that Volkswagen could do such a thing. The CEO had to resign. He did. At the time he left he got an estimated $ 60 million. Cool.

Nokia failed. The CEO cried (tears) during the last press conference and said "Nokia did nothing wrong but we lost". He got a $ 24 million send-off while a lot of Finns lost their jobs. He took the million-dollar bonus anyway. His wife divorced him. Maybe she understood the situation better.

I am sure you have heard of Rajaratinam and his elite network that made it a cakewalk for him to indulge in insider trading and super profits in short time. Some are notoriously brilliant and the rest of us follow the rules. I have heard of his insider trading but have not as yet heard of him sharing a wee bit of his wealth. That might have made him a Robin Hood of sorts! Rajaratinam is in jail along with Rajat who one time was with McKinsey Consulting.

The biggest problem with capitalism is cronyism. The top 'leadership' rakes it in and in times of crisis more often than not the buck stops at the lower levels. The top protects each other and take millions in bonuses, equity and whatever.

Like in Wells Fargo where its own customers were given accounts they didn't need and charged money for transactions that were not required. The guys at the bottom are being blamed. And not a single guy who took in those millions was aware of what was happening behind their bottoms? Incredible. Rip off your own customers and take not a shred of the blame.

Wells Fargo CEO was on record to state the problem was not as grave as the senate thought it was.

Later he resigned from the company taking with him a nine figure package-an estimated $ 133 million.

I am not at all being moral about it. Some of these figures include pension and shares accumulated during their tenure. All I can say is that the growing divide and the widening gap between the very rich and the rest created a Trump. I need not say more.

If you don't share you go down. One more time nature will teach us this lesson in 2017-2020.

Yet again. Yet one more time.

Spread the wealth. To the have nots. The cosmos means business. And we all better listen.

When corporates made super profits did they give it back not only to their shareholders but stakeholders and the community in equal measure? Actually, it is economic common sense and doesn't need an MBA to figure out that money spread over a population, goes around and keeps the engines of a community humming. Concentrated in a few hands it is useless.

When banks offered you loans did they eye only their own chart busting profits? There is a problem when banks rush in and give loans. No matter what. Banks give loans whether you want it or not. And if its Wells Fargo it gives you accounts you don't need.

When big corporates showed signs of default were they categorized as such in the balance sheet or were they hidden under some accounting jargon. Which means when the banks showed profit they were actually in loss. Did they hide it?

When large corporates defaulted, were the loans collected or worse were more loans offered. This is a problem not endemic to Asia as we thought. Though it is changing there as well. Some big fish use whatever rules, laws and clauses or hidden text. Or shift their money to tax havens. And some small fish caught in the EMI net struggle. To break free.

Isn't there a wide gap between the so many people who just about earn and just have just enough and those who are very rich? In the USA, there is vast number of people who are not satisfied about their salaries. There is a clear divide between the rich and the rest.

Cornerstone Macro technical analyst Carter Worth told CNBC's "Fast Money" traders."When you see the relative performance of utilities, bonds and the S&P 500 index acting opposite to each other, you're about to get another contraction."

The correlation between these three factors as well as gold and corporate bonds was analyzed. Carter stated that each divergence and contraction took place during periods of recession.

Not only has he predicted a deep recession but goes on to say: "It's very hard to reverse it."

Economic destiny is a pet theme of this book.

'The results of every action are etched at the time of the action itself.'

The world's best are trying all they can and more. Every trick and every tactic. And find that it all spills up in their faces.

Economics is destiny.

Destiny puts you in your place. If you have done right, you will be in the right place. If you have done wrong, you will be in the wrong place. Everyone should be ethical while earning money. Because destiny has a way of catching up.

The FDA has fined 14 billion dollars to Deutsche bank for mortgage security fraud.

Wells Fargo rips off its own customers. And is facing the music, including a class action suit by its own employees. Six employees filed a case against Wells Fargo on behalf of all employees who were fired or demoted for refusing to open fake accounts.

One fraud after another. By someone we trust.

Will Deutsche Bank be the Lehman Bros of 2017?

At the time we decide we need to decide right. At the time we act we need to act right.

VOODOO & THE ARMAGEDDON

Global economics is global destiny.

Central banks are running 'out of ammunition'.

CNN Money 9 Feb 2016

'They're pumping money into their economies, creating negative interest rates and buying billions of dollars in bonds. Yet experts are worried these strategies will not be enough to turn around the slump in the world.'

"As soon as the markets realize that the Fed and the ECB are out of ammunition, it's over," Stockman said. "I think we're in an extremely unsafe world — we've never been here before."

This is by a former US government Director of Budget.

'We are getting into a place where we have never been before.'

The Armageddon.

They were manufacturing cash out of thin air. The voodoo economists.

It failed in Japan and it failed in USA.

QE1 was useful. We should have bitten the bullet then. QE2 and QE3 were largely pumping money that was used to create a sense of well being. Like being on steroids. This was creating a bubble burst for recession and all indicators pointed towards a depression.

However China has now initiated measures to tighten and buck up its economy. USA is taking some steps towards kick starting something positive. Spain is a bright spot (though with persisting weakness), a beacon to economic recovery. Deutsche bank has initiated corrective action. Will all these add up or is it too late?

Will USA survive the interest rate hikes? Not just stopping the easy money but indeed reversal and tightening money policy is like thermal heat followed by cold freezing.

The interest rate are cumulative. Every 0.25 hike adds to the previous and the cumulative weight bears down on the economy. In fact the a 2017 survey of the most influential global money managers put interest rate hike as the second most possible cause of a recession. Just below the trade wars.

The trade war is hanging like a Damocles Sword. Just in Mar-2017 China warned USA that it would retaliate in case USA started a tariff war. China clearly stated the 1930s would be revisited in case this happened. They were referring to the trade war that culminated in the greatest depression that capitalism has ever seen.

The meet between Trump and China is already scheduled and is just weeks away. The tenor of the meet will reverberate through 2017-2020.

THE BABY BOOMERS – OUT OF ACTION

In 1989 Japan reached the height of its economy. Today Japan is just another lagging economy trying to find its bearings. It's home to an ageing economically inactive population.

USA today is facing a similar issue. The disappearance of the baby boomer generation – the bulk of its generation driving the economy – buying, investing and entrepreneuing. In the USA this generation controls 4 times the GDP of its country. It's these economically active people, actually an economic powerhouse that were responsible for the greatest economic activity through the 70's, 80's and 90's; that are entering into retirement hibernation. A major chunk of peak household spending is going to go out. The US government states 'This will have a profound economic effect.' It's simple – People are at the core of the economy; people move the economy.

When active people become inactive a part of the economy moves from activity to inactivity.

UTILITY

Availability of cash created an economy which did not have real utility. People created coz they had money not coz they had use or need for it. So you had ghost cities. Which fuelled a ghost economy and people didn't know of it until it became a ghostly news story.

The last trick was QE. QE was useful initially. In large part the QE had outlived its utility. Did the central banks carry out an analysis of the utility of QE every six months or every year?

No. They just had a blind shot.

But from now on the Cosmos will put utility on center stage. Right up there.

The fetal cities of China. The 'city planners', the 'masters of economy' the false creations of the commodity boom, the exports boom in several countries. The unborn cities will ring in the death knell of the modern mismanaged economy. We should not build cities that will not be populated. Violation of the crucial economic principle: Utility.

Do something useful that will be used.

A fitness program that promotes health.

A preacher who is sincere.

A banker who gives a loan which gives ROI.

A clinical research which results in a drug that cures.

A goldsmith who crafts a design which is aesthetic.

A builder who designs a city which is smart.

An economist whose policy alleviates poverty.

A leader who implements.

A movie that people enjoy to watch.

An assassination which is globally applauded.

All these have utility. They are useful. They can be used. People will flock to them even in a recession.

Why do I say all this? It seems to be pretty obvious. But much happens in the world that on hindsight seems so very foolish.

More than a 1000 clinical trials were recently rejected due to dubious data. We all know of leaders who never implement. We have seen movies which we didn't enjoy. We have had wars which didn't serve a purpose.

While in theory doing right, doing well and doing the best seems to be just natural; in reality we find decisions and events can be downright gross.

So if we are the ones who stand up and in whatever domain we are in we can justly say I am of utility (quality, consistency, expertise, knowledge, information and delivery) people will flock to us even in a recession.

Do our world leaders and economist and bankers need to be taught this basic lesson of human economic behavior − Utility?

In our frenzy a penchant has grown, a temptation to make the simple convoluted.

Making life complicated we have tied ourselves in a complex web that we are unable to get out of. Risky complicated derivatives and other financial products so convoluted that we just don't get it.

The more the convoluted the more the genius?

Actually the more seamlessly simple it seems, the more the genius.

A genius simplifies the complex.

E = MC Square.

Simple. Utility.

RECESSION : THE SURVIVAL GUIDE.

Finally we are here. What can you do? As individuals. Because governments will not be able to do much. In fact may not be able to do anything at all.

Here are some solutions, some measures that you can pick and choose. Choose the best options. The ones that suit you, that make sense to you.

Here we go.

What should I Do? I.

"Only I can Act. Now."

1. Skill yourself: Make yourself useful and more useful at whatever level you are in. Get that much better. Domain skill, technical skill, networking skill, service skill, communication skill…Do right to yourself. Then do right to your community. Then you might find yourself in the right place when you meet catastrophe face to face.

2. Compact: One Person Business. If you can manage a business alone then you can float. Use tech, use e-comm, use gadgets. That will cut down cost of employees (you can take home the salary of every person you don't employee). And using online somewhere can possibly cut down on realty space.

3. Family Business: The profit goes to the family.

4.Cost: Can you service a demand at lesser cost. Obviously cost will be a significant determinant. Right on top.

5. Practice agriculture. You will be assured of food, housing and health. The small farm house. Being with nature and working on the farm is as healthy as it can get. And food can be a business.

Agriculture is one of Jim Rogers favorite. Mine too. In fact this can be one of the most safest and even profitable if you can think of it in that way during a crisis. But remember agriculture is not just farming. Be innovative. Be different to make a difference. There can be as many product variants in the agri - food space as in the new car launches. But then if at some time you want to get away from it all, then farming is just what the doctor ordered.

6. Urban planting.

Use LED light as a substitute for sunlight. LED plants require 10 times less space and but give a high yield.

Soiless planting. Mineralized water that supply just the minerals that are need. No soil.

So there, in a small space you have all the nutritious food you would ever want. It may not matter if the sun rises the next day or not.

You may start a home delivery of essential food.

7. Community: This is vital. Be a vibrant community. Just don't look at the size. The community has to be vibrant. The support system.

WhatsApp with an extended live ecosystem. That will keep your spirits afloat and high. We cannot just survive we can live during a recession! The colors of a community become our colors. Be a prominent part of a community of common as well as strategic interests.

8. Gold. One of Wall Street's most accurate forecasters JP Morgan's Kolanovic predicts that stocks markets are in trouble. His choice of investment is gold.

The CEO of Euro Pacific Capital says the U.S. economy is in the midst of a recession that could turn out to be even more horrible than the Great Recession of 2008. He is confident of only this option: Gold. The safe haven. But buy on dips.

It does make sense however to keep a portion of investment in different asset classes. Current scenario for gold is quite complicated. In Dec 2016 when the Fed increased the interest rate gold was down by 5-10%. And Trump mania was all over corporate USA. The superhero would get them super profits. And gold was pummeled. And with at least 2 and even 3 interest rate increases expected in 2017 there could be enough pressure to take gold down. But then Trump behaving at the borderline of sensibility — ejecting journalist from a press meet, heated argument with the Mexican president and a shout out with the Australian PM and seriously the trade wars — the fears of a Trump goof up is in itself a strong positive for gold. So, in the short term there are as many positive as negative signals for gold. The short term fluctuation is complicated and gold could go very much down. In long term though you would want it in your kitty.

Why gold? Instinctively we all will rush for it.

So, if you must then

: Buy on large dips (just prior to a widely expected fed rate increase)

: Buy with a longer term outlook (holding it for 3-5 years and not looking at the price of it again every now and then).

Have a portion for saving — a 3-5 year outlook - and a portion for trading. And if you get a target profit in the short term then you could sell and book profit with the trading portion. It could be volatile and you might get a chance to pick it up at a lower level.

9. Some experts plump for dollars. Their advice is to purchase dollars. Jim Rogers is betting for Dollars against other currencies.

Jim Rogers buys into dollars in 2016 not because it has inherent strength but because lot of people believe it to be strong and will buy it. Or it may be the only one of the few options available when all else is sinking. A place to stay put for sometime. And now with Trump the dollar is getting stronger day by day. Dollar it is for now. But by the time you read this we are in 2017 and dollar might have got overcrowded.

10. Place. Where you will be, stay and earn will matter the most.

If you wish to stay reasonable by the end of 2017 then plan to head to the few places in the world that are relatively untouched.

UNESCO has voted him the best PM in the world. India. This country has rallied behind one of the few world leaders worth his salt. Who says what he means and means what he says. Backed by the governor of their central bank they have one of the fastest real growths currently. They are investing in roads, trains and housing. They have recovered billions of dollars of 'stashed cash' from their own citizens!

Indonesia. Or the few such countries. South East Asia.

11. If you can't head there then consider investing in some Asian economies.

Asia Focused Funds (AFF). Get in touch with them. Seek out the financial data of the country. Compare the financial parameters and Invest.

Debt, Debt to GDP ratio, Growth Rate. The basics will give an idea.

Seek out sectors and companies that profit from internal business.

Check for companies that are focused on emerging core technologies and emerging technologies.

Spread your investment among sectors and companies.

Financial indicators as EPS and PE (versus historical and peer values) can give a fair idea of the companies you plan to invest in. If you want to dig deeper you can go into debt-equity ratio, percentage of other income in the profit, project orders in hand and so on.

The way you invest and manage will be different. Ask your financial advisor some pointed questions. If you see him squirm then maybe you asked him right.

But do enquire about upcoming investment and projects. Biosimilars, robotics, electric cars, renewable energy, cloud computing, data analytics, e-com, VR, digital and so on. Online ventures and AI startups before you know can be all over the place. What is happening now and in the near future. Mix the current and the future (current and future profit). Go for it.

12. Lithium and Cobalt the 'fuel' of electric cars. And graphene. The new age wonder. These can take off. That is obvious.

13. As per a recent survey people who live in Denmark, Norway, Sweden and Switzerland are the happiest in the world. Don't worry. Be happy. Head to Holland.

It's a chance to have an adventure.

Escape to happy countries. Immigrate.

14. Stay in A Forest. Yes. This is a serious option. Deep in the forest. Or near habitation. In a tree house. Make it safe whichever you choose. You can live out your fantasies. And you may have the best time of your life. An adventure you only dreamed about.

15. Hobby. Take up that hobby that you always dreamt of and you many find a treasure within yourself. Now that you may have time. Don't think about ROI for this year. See how liberating that can be. By the way have you heard of Charles Darrow and a hobby? Read on.

16. Write a diary. It can be a surprising perspective a side of yourself you didn't know existed. Some diaries have gone on to become bestsellers. The grit the survival the pleasures and happiness even in the adversity the enduring spirit of human life.

17. SSP : Did ever your financial advisor tell you about SSP. The Systematic Selling Plan?

Horse with blinkers. Many a times education makes us see only what we have been trained to. It makes us blind to the reality which is all around us.

In Feb 2016 the stocks were down. In Oct 2016 the stocks again went down. Over the course of next year there could be a sell off. Or at the very least, times when the stocks will be down. Every year has a high and a low for a stock. Just look at the PE and that can give an indication for the sell signal. However you also need to be aware of the current market scenario and therefore have regular discussions with a group as well as your financial advisor. Do get some inputs regarding the performance of your company, the order wins, the last couple of month sales before taking a buy or sell decision. Just a 10 minute online search and browse is enough to get you that information. And you will be surprised at the accuracy of your own decision and your understanding of market dynamics.

Browse 'The Motley Fool.' He has beaten the experts hollow when it comes to stock picking and market profit. We are also the motley fools and we can beat the experts.

If you are in profit or have reached a target price then SSP makes perfect sense. Sell systematically every time the stocks rise, you can pick them at a lower price when the stocks go down or you can book the profit and watch it go down all the way. But if it goes up and you have made your target profit and you would still be satisfied. There are other stocks that are about to make a move.

It is likely that when Trump announces the corporate tax cuts Dow Jones will reach its zenith for 2017. I reckon that is the time to get out of USA stocks. Sell during euphoria.

Warren Buffet has a rumored $ 55 billion in cash. What about you?

Try SSP.

If a recession starts in Euro-Japan then the US stocks may go up very high before crashing. But in the event of Trump failing to deliver then it could be a reaction that takes it down straight for maybe a big correction of 10 - 25 percent.

But so much depends on upcoming decisions. Trump talks of tariff. Just for a moment imagine he does actually walk the talk.

To what extent tariffs will be initiated and the ramifications range from mild to downright scary.

If Trump does not learn from Hoover then he does not learn from history. If we don't learn from history and a tariff war culminates into a trade war we may all live to regret it.

What if Trump does not announce the tax breaks in 2017?

What if the healthcare bill ends up in a mess?

That's why I insist the future is unpredictable. And the Dow keeps going up as if it's a smooth ride ahead. The dangers are big and potent. The dangers are real. The future is really unpredictable.

The range of the swing is huge and unpredictable.

A recession can bring down anything but cannot stop the advance in technology.

A recession is not about selling. It is about selling first and buying later at 50 % down levels.

It is a mistake to think that recession is forever. There have been legends born due to, during and after the 1929 depression. But then you need to know which stock to pick, which trade to do and which talent to hone.

Did you know that the average recession last about a couple of years and bull markets keep going for years?

Were there no rich people during the great depression of 1929 and were there no one who became rich due to the depression?

It's not only about survival. Getty became a Rockfeller only because of the great depression. It can open up unseen possibilities − Be alert to ever changing scenario. Get ready for the roller coaster ride. And if you make the right decisions at the right time you will end on the top of the wave. If you think we are talking only money here then you are dead wrong.

We are talking of life. And there is more to life than just money. Read on.

People will just prefer to celebrate the forest life or write a diary of this rare time of 2017 some will downright be focused on the funds the SSP and the AFF and others will mix and match the options such as community and home agri and make it a part of their lifestyle.

Whatever you choose to do, it is about time you start.

The better prepared cope better.

Remember recessions last a couple of years and booms go on for years.

The King and His Preacher.

Let me tell you the story of a king who invited his preacher for a hunt. Armed with bows, arrows and spears the huntsmen enter the forest. Deep inside the dense forest amidst large gnarled trees and thick creepers the sounds of the wild keep the huntsmen on the alert. After he has had his turn, the king points towards boar and offers the preacher a gilded bow and arrow.

"Go for it preacher."

The preacher says "Hey King. I am a preacher. What would I know about hunting?"

The King replies "Try your luck good preacher. Who knows you might get it just right. The Bulls Eye. Ha, Ha."

The preacher moves back, tries to position himself as he can and let's go. It's pure disaster.

The arrow has gone haywire and has pierced the king's arm.

Angered by this the king orders the preacher to the dungeons while he himself driven by a royal thirst for adventure carries on with the hunt.

But then, there is danger lurking around the corner. A downswing in the life of the king. Cannibals await their next meal and the king walks right into the cannibal tribe while many of his soldiers escape into the wilderness.

Just as they are about to fry the king one of them notices the open gash on the kings arm. Afraid of bad omen they refuse to consider the king as food and release him.

The king rushes back to his palace, heads to the dungeons and hugs the preacher.

"Preacher. If you had not injured me with the misaimed arrow and had I not this wound on my arm the cannibals would have found me to be perfect and would have fried me in burning oil. Thanks to you, I am alive today!"

"Your Kingship. Had you not put me in the dungeons I would have still accompanied you. The cannibals finding me without any injury would have selected me as their food. Thanks to you, I am alive today!"

A downswing in our lives. We may get hurt maybe even badly but then it may be for the good. I am sure it can be if we take some sensible steps.

LIMPID EYED COSMOS

I had a bit cosmos hugging me today. Looking at me with limpid eyes. I was carrying her. She will save me from the harsh world. My 2 year girl going onto 3. Just about making sense of the world. But not touched by it. Hug your own cosmos, support them; they will be your saviors. When you look at their expectant innocent eyes and face you get a sense of belongingness. Yes we belong to someone. That is the essence of our existence.

But then we will need to look beyond those who belong to us. Just in case we have forgotten in the hurry to reach our targets.

Our targets will now reach as low as they can get and give us all the time we need to learn that interwoven is our life and we need to reach out to every human we come across in as natural a manner that nature ordained human behavior to be.

It seems apt to end where it all began. Targets.

What is your target? 'Your.'

What is the target of humanity? 'Humanity'.

You achieve your targets.

And allow humanity to achieve its.

What is humanity's target. Money, business, profit at any cost ?

Humane. Be humane. All the time.

At any meet. At any conference. Any decision. Every pitch. Every tactic. Every strategy.

Be humane.

The End Result.

Generate profit at any cost ? "Ha Ha."

SUCCESS STORIES

Darrow : Driven out of work by the great depression Charles Darrow spent time in designing a game that went on to be called Monopoly. It became so popular that the first ever game designer millionaire was created.

Getty : He inherited 5,00,000 dollars. When the stocks crashed he bought oil stocks at their lowest level. J Paul Getty held on for a long enough time to become the first billionaire of the great depression.

Kennedy: Joe Kennedy made his money in the stock market and got out at the right times to invest in real estate and movie studios to stay rich for more time.

You can become rich in the stock market. But to stay rich you need to know when to get out. Get out before the others do.

Cullen : Cullen worked in the retail market. He gave an idea that his bosses rejected. He went out on a limb and worked out his idea that ultimately made him 75 million dollars.

You have an idea you believe in. Recessions and depressions are just great times to work out ideas that have been rejected.

Cagney: James Cagney went from $500 to $40000 a week. Depressions have been extremely fertile ground for creatives. Legends have been born.

What are you waiting for?

As the man who pulverized the great depression of 1929 famously said : 'You have only fear to fear.' FDR.

It's not only about the money, baby.

Script Your Success.

WHEN IT DOES REVIVE

AS IT WILL

THE

CATACLYSMIC CHANGES

WILL BE

AKIN

TO THE

METAMORPHOSIS

OF A

CATERPILLAR INTO A BUTTERFLY.

In the early 1900 those who were affluent had iceboxes. A horse drawn carriage would stop by to deliver ice everyday. Until refrigerators were invented. Not long back the night was lit by lamps until electricity was discovered. Civilization changed. Time was when letters took days to reach your feelings to your loved ones. SMS does it in an instant. Reality seems magical.

Our children will live in a world they did not grow up in. Drones, hyperloop speed, personalized gene based medical therapy, anti-ageing, robots, facial recognition, chatbots, flying cars (yes they will come much before self driving cars), third dimension of reality and super-technology that will once again change the screen saver of history and make the world so different than it was ever before.

Humankind will emerge once again.

The Last Thoughts

A falling value pinches everyone. A tiger grows cat's whiskers.

The indicators are the result.

Be humane. Don't rip off your own customers.

Zero interest rate regimes has led to over-production.

A consumption not driven by need contributes to the formation of a bubble.

That economy which circulates within reasonable limits spikes within reasonable limits. And the economy which crosses all limits crashes without limit.

Wal-Mart, Macys, Sears close hundreds of stores laying of tens of thousands of workers.

Search for places to hide. To escape the avalanche of the economic downswing.

Live at the fringe. Get the best of both the worlds.

Live at the fringe. Get the best of the forest and get away from the worst of the city.

Trump. Trade wars And The Great Fall Of China.

Chinese real estate magnate Wang Jianlin has stated that "Residential real estate in China is now the biggest bubble in history." One prick and the blast will wipe off a third of GDP.

Torsten Slok who works as a chief international economist has a chart which shows that China's credit bubble exceeded even that of USA on the edge of subprime mortgage meltdown that led into the 2008 recession.

Mar 2017: China central bank head states the China debt is a huge concern and they must bring it down quickly. China debt is 260 %.

All this without a trade war.

If a trade war starts? Absolute Terror.

In 2017 China actually warns USA that it should not forget the 1930 trade war that started it all.

South China Sea and the domination streak of Chin.

China aspires to be the world leader.

We will have ample time to think about this as the events unfold before our seemingly unbelieving eyes.

The culprits are the banks. They give 'easy' money. And expect it back.

Did the banks think that people will borrow from them and make profits out of a tentative economy?

And pay them back for the banks to enjoy super profits! How dreamy! Or delusional ?

It will begin with the banks. And extend everywhere.

Uninvest to Reinvest.

Banks or casinos?

When banks become casinos the economy is a gamble.

126   The moon is a safe place. I will go there. Because there are no banks on the moon.

The stats are staggeringly negative.

The Stoxx last reached its high in 2000. Since then it has been hitting lower highs.

Right now the Stoxx has formed a shoulder-head-shoulder pattern.

And the projection is a lower high sometime in the last quarter of 2017 and 2018.

The signals from Eurozone are the color Red.

QE: When everything fails we fall back on magic. Close your eyes. Open now. Hey we have more money ! The voodoo economics of the voodoo economists.

Be brave and bite the bullet. We should have. The last chance was missed.

The End Result is an extrapolation of the initial decision multiplied by a factor.

The End Result is Upon Us.

This time the recession will teach us to be humane.

To purge the wild excesses, the panicky decisions, the irrational behavior, the greedy clinging and the selfish motivations and cowardly attitude.

Be ready for fly by wire decisions.

There will be minimal government intervention. Coz governments have done all they could. And have no more tricks in the bag.

Nature has given us many years and more opportunities to take effective action. But when we don't, it steps in and makes sure we pay for the economic blunders we have committed.

We have a downswing. Look up. Someone up there may know what he is doing. Read 'The King And The Preacher'.

Marks And Spencer shuts down a 100 stores. A 100...!!!

15 Nov 2016. French PM: "Europe on brink of Collapse"

When the indicators are bad the result cannot be good.

Economic indicators are like health indicators. When you have a bad lab test then surely there must be a bad disease that led to it.

Indicators are precursors of results. We can't have bad indicators and a good result. We can't have increased troponins and wish that the heart is normal.

When the indicators are bad the result will be bad. And right now the indicators are quite bad.

Global economy is global destiny.

The precision of the universe is at play.

Forget the community; forget the climate; forget the have nots. Let's just achieve targets.

"Ha.Ha."

Nature and Humaneness will together have the last laugh.

"Ha.Ha."

Average Americans have not been saving enough. The haves have it and the have nots do not have it. The gap between them is wide.

Government may be the reason for the recession? Because they bailed out the big banks with public money. And big banks created a speculative bubble of derivates 30 times the size of the US debt – more than $ 500 trillion of derivatives.

Did we talk about executives who own islands while there are millions who can barely rent a shelter.

The haves and the have nots. Is this all about this ?

But there is much more to Trump if nearly half of America has voted for someone against distinguished rivals. Trump must surely have touched the core of peoples' aspirations. No doubt.

Lots of people not employed. Lots of people with less salary. Lots of people with less savings. Lots of people with more expenses. Lots of people on the other side. Lots of have nots. USA Today. They have elected Trump. They are watching Trump. He better do something great.

Sometimes it seems like Trump may be the only one who was ever capable of taking the bull by the horns.

The initial days are the honeymoon days. We all know what happens in the later part of a marriage. The next page – Experience marriage: raw and hard core.

If not for anything just for the high PE get out of US stocks by Mar-Apr 2017.

It's not Trump. It's a trumpet.

It is people like Anouseh Ansari that have forced Trump to leave out Iran from the list of banned countries.

The healthcare bill fails.

All talk and no output makes Jack a Trump.

Trump cannot pass bills. Government business will be at standstill. Do you know what that means? I hope you do for your own sake.

USA will be caught in the crossfire between Trump, his own party non-supporters, opposition party and the Fed.

Will USA survive Trump? Will an already divided USA come together again?

Will Trump manage to swing USA? So far so good. Because it is all hope and not performance?

If Trump starts a trade war it will be the last nail in the coffin.

Will we be the destined witness of an Economic Downswing?

The Last Quarter Of 2017...Oct 2017. The Downswing.

Sometimes the best comes out of the worst. Hope that we are in that situation.

What we have been doing is against humanity's target. And there lies the crux of the problem and the biggest lesson the Cosmos is trying to teach us though the coming crash.

It is nature's way of purging excess and dead sloth greed from its system. Nature and the real economy don't like these. Small relief.

There is Life beyond ROI.

A must read for everyone to know how the global economy arrived at the mess it is in.

131 A small spark starts a jungle fire when the twigs are dry and many.

The precision of the universe is at play.

Forget the community; forget the climate; forget the have nots. Let's just achieve targets.

"Ha.Ha."

Nature and Humaneness will together have the last laugh.

"Ha.Ha."

Basically it is about the basics. Basics are the foundation. Basics are the building blocks. Basics are all there is. Basic is the end point.

You get the basic right you get everything right.

You decide your future at the time you act.

Useful plus Used = Effective.

Utilize every moment. These will never come back.

Moments are all you have.

The next two years will reveal that utility is linked to survival.

Charles Darwin's Survival of the Fittest will be successfully tested once again.

Someone who is skilled is always of value. Those who are useful will be used. And will be paid for the use.

Even in a recession people will visit a restaurant that serves tasty nutritious food, to watch that movie which is entertaining and go to that doctor who gives accurate diagnosis.

Compact: This will make a strong comeback.

Compact and utility will go hand in hand.

Warren Buffet has a name for derivatives. He calls them Weapons of Mass Destruction.

We are in the third largest expansion in the history of capitalism. One of the longest in recent memories started in the 1990's and ended in the dot com bust. There have been 33 recessions in the history of capitalism. The longest expansion has lasted 10 years and the average duration of an expansion is 5 years. We are currently running 8 years. Are we due for the next one between 2017-2020? Maybe late 2017 when Trump would be reassessed by corporate America and the rest of the world? Will it be the failure of Trump policies or a war or war like situation in South China sea or North Korea that will trigger a domino effect on an already weak Euro - Japan - South American geography? Or will it be the crash of the bad Euro banks that will pull in Japan and USA. Or will there be a few more Toshiba Nuclear that will one day reveal they are no more.

To escape the effects of the 2008 QE was started. Pump in easy money. With no real demand. By not withdrawing QE and taking their medicine in 2012 – market imbalances today are now bigger and the consequences greater.

The culprits are the central banks (though they are not the only ones). This is where they started giving cash to create the cash illusion.

1929 Lets go back and take a look.

In the great depression of 1929 were there no rich people. Yet for every wealthy guy every there were thousands holding the food bowl.

Where do you want to be in 2017. How to get to where you want to be in 2017.

Make a decision based on facts. Take a considered opinion.

Belongingness gives us the strength to carry on against all odds. The more we enlarge our belongingness the more humane we will be.

It's a game. The game is on. It can affect. It's real. Play it well. It is not static.

Be alert.

Situations will be dynamic.

Subscribe to read.

Spend at least 10 mins a day to watch targeted news.

Get alerts to your Whatsapp.

Timing is crucial. High stakes games. Very crucial.

Small steps but big stakes!

Whatsapp for entertainment. Now use Whatsapp for the game of your life. Join or create a group. Get real time news and flashes.

We cannot just survive we can live during a recession! The colors of a community become our colors.

Have a meaningful conversation with your financial advisor. Ask and engage him.

Sell stocks. If you don't want to do it all at once, the other option is to do it with a SSP.

Everytime your stocks go up. Download. So that you get the best average price. But start now.

The situation will be dynamic. It is important to know when to buy and more important to know when to sell.

Hobby. We can discover facets to life hitherto hidden. That can be fascinating. And you can be the Charles Darrow of 2017 !

Forest – Nature. We can discover facets to life hitherto hidden. That can be fascinating.

If you are in profit it is time to download stocks now. Systematic Selling Plan.

Follow the legends.

Accumulate the safe haven metals on dips. Lithium and Cobalt are the new and spectacular 'precious metal' and on the other end is gold the perennial safe haven. Consider graphene – the new kid on the block.

Focus on South Asian funds

Immigrate to happy countries

Reach out to me.

More millionaires were made due to the great depression than at other times.

Happiness is a byproduct of attitude. Improve your attitude.

One step in the right direction gives the strength for two steps in the right direction. Two steps in the right direction gives the strength for 4 steps in the right direction. 4 steps... Just substitute the word right with wrong and see where you end up.

Economy will now have to be managed with an eye on cause and effect. Whatever we do will comeback to us with a multiplier. Are we just pumping money (QE) into the system. What are the actual effects? Are the actions of the central banks the answer to combat the 2008 recession or was it just a patch up to leave us vulnerable to bigger disasters. We will know in the coming few years. If this is the way to manage a recession then recessions can be managed. We would have devised a mechanism. But if it pans out like more than a few are predicting that this might lead to bigger problems and bigger downturns, then we have to rethink. If we have a chance to rethink, that is.

The Direction Of The Future.

AI and robotics are evolving fast, under the radar. They have reached escape velocity.

Follow the tech trend. A recession can stop everything but not the advance of technology. If there is one medicine that can cure a recession it is a tech wave. Identify and Invest in the tech trend before it becomes a tech wave.

If you have the tech bug then times are such if you invest your time the tech bug can become a tech career and take you places.

Top 20 Tech Predictions 2017

https://www.thestreet.com/story/13925845/1/top-10-tech-stock-predictions-for-2017.html

Gartner estimates the market for BI and analytics at USD 22.8 billion by 2020. Modern BI (business intelligence) and analytics continue to expand.

Invest your money, your time, your skill set and even your career. In the direction of the future.

Imagine the time when there were no cities. We lived in the forest. We lived.

When Greece collapsed the banks in Greece were closed. People had to line up at ATMs for their daily ration of fixed money.

A survivor said: Parents dream for their kids. I live a nightmare and see my children foraging garbage for food.

Stay at the fringe of a forest where the city ends. And the recession can be an adventure in a tree house. And you can live.

Get the best of air, water and fruits and enter the city to do what you have to do. But come back to the fringe where the city meets the forest. For this is the place where ... you can live.

You won't need electricity because the moonlight will be there to take care of you and all that you wear.

THE QUOTES

"I think we're in an extremely unsafe (economic) world — we've never been here before." The former director of the Office of Management and Budget, Stockman. Stockman has been a lynchpin of the US government during its heydays.

"A lot of the problems in the investment bank have been that people have been trying to generate revenue at all costs." Thiam, CEO Credit Suisse.

Generate revenue at any cost."Ha Ha."- Piam, Publisher.

Between Trump, the Fed and the Senate I get an image of a mashed potato — Piam.

In 2017 economics will make history.

The center of gravity will start to shift to the East.

East Ho ! West No !

Solar energy production will grow exponentially as cost comes down. If we get to air travel on alternative energy that will be the end of oil as the major source of transport energy that connects existence.

An electric airplane has been tested and it lasted 10 minutes in air. Regional EV air connectivity is near.

If we achieve oil-less aerospace then we are through for eternity – or at least as long as the sun lasts.

In 50 years from now humans will squeeze the last drop of oil from the bowels of the Earth.

PWC estimates that India would overtake USA to become the 2nd largest economy in the world in the next 2 decades. Catch the growth. Be in India.

Brand is a brand coz of its value. The value of a brand may be tested this year. There may be more value in non brands. Identify these and you have what is called a multibagger in stocks. Is the brand worth the value – is not a question that consumers will be asking all the time. But when they do it reflects on the stock value too.

PWC states that emerging nations will overtake developed countries in the coming decade and India will overtake USA as an economic superpower.

Anousheh Ansari the first woman private space traveler. An engineer. She is from Iran.

175 Global CIO and PM Survey – 2017

Protectionist policies could be the catalyst that may be the end of the 8-year global equity bull market. This is a BofA-ML's latest monthly survey of 175 global chief investment officers and portfolio managers. They together manage $543 billion in assets and this is their opinion.

Trade Wars: 34%
High Interest Rates: 28%
Unpredictable Financial Event: 18%
Weak Earning: 18%

Thirty four percent felt it would be the trade wars while Twenty eight per cent felt that higher interest rates could bring back the bears.

EM equities found favor with global funds. 49 per cent of them said EM equities were undervalued (so we need to head to the emerging markets). So there we have it form the horses' mouth.

The LAST WORD

It will start with the interest rate hike. Stocks will crash. Real estate will join in.

It will start when the QE ends.

It will start with the Euro banks. Taking down Italy, Greece spreading like a contagion through Europe, Japan. USA has its own set of issues that are enough and interconnected for it to fall like never before witnessed in the history of humans.

Or is it a war like situation - the South China sea, the aggressive bans polarizing a community, providing fodder for spread of more radical sentiments or is it the renegade North Korea that will spook the world.

Will USA survive Trump? Will an already divided USA come together again?

Is a Recession staring at us?

Then Trump comes along and there is corporate hope.

Employment rates are up and nonfarm payrolls in USA are encouraging in the very first month of 2017.

The Trump policies have sent Dow on a record high and corporate America is gung ho.

China is showing inclination to stabilize.

UK is fine as of now inspite of Brexit (or due to it?)

South Asia is vibrant.

And Tech is on a journey that can change the world.

Is Supernormal staring at us?

Will it be a recession − normal − supernormal ?

THE FUTURE IS UNPREDICTABLE.

AND WE NEED A STRATEGY TO DEAL WITH IT.

It makes sense to have a strategy.

No war was won without one.

The Piam Investment Strategy

For Investment today is not less than a war.

The Dow keeps breaking records. And the best time to book profits is fast approaching - Mar 2017. By then the markets will have a glimpse of Trump's ability or lack of it. If the markets realize that tax breaks are not coming in 2017 and they already have had interest rate hike with possible more hikes, they will tank. If Trump does announce a budget with the tax breaks or the $1 trillion investment and it meets expectations Dow will soar. That will be the best time in a long time the best time to book profits. And get away. From then on it will be performance and not hope that will guide the Dow.

Trump on Trump Policy
10-year Economic Effect: Plus 1.5% a year
10 - year debt impact : Nil (!!!)
Assumes trade, immigration and regulatory positives.

Tax Policy Center
10 year Economic Growth: -0.5% a year
10 year debt impact: Plus $7 trillion
Factors interest rate hike due to increase in deficit

Moody's
10 - year Economic Growth: -1.7% a year
10 year debt impact: Plus $13 trillion.
Factors in trade policy and interest rate hike due to higher deficit.

From:http://time.com/money/4584852/trump-tax-plan-deficit-buster/

See, other than Trump himself others are not quite cheerful about his policies. He scores negative on economic impact and adds more to the debt as per the external calculations.

Trump says his policies won't add a penny to the debt.

Hmm. Is it Trump or a trumpet?

THE LINKS

Top 30 Valuable Brands 2017
http://www.msn.com/en-in/money/photos/top-30-most-valuable-brands-of-2017/ss-AAmBqiA?li=AAggbRN&ocid=SK2CDHP#image=22

Top Emerging Market 2017
https://www.bloomberg.com/news/articles/2017-01-02/top-investor-picks-for-emerging-markets-in-2017

Stratfor 2017 Annual Forecast.
https://www.stratfor.com/forecast/2017-annual-forecast

Worlds 10 Happiest Countries (In Pics)
https://www.forbes.com/pictures/geeg45edkjh/1-denmark/#3e0727be7ae1

Black Scholes : Equation of the 2008 Recession
https://www.theguardian.com/science/2012/feb/12/black-scholes-equation-credit-crunch

Top 20 Tech Predictions 2017
https://www.thestreet.com/story/13925845/1/top-10-tech-stock-predictions-for-2017.html

What you get depends on how the globe is doing. It's therefore your business to know about the globe.

The book that everyone should read so that they know where they stand.

Because where you stand may not be safe.

The book to guide you through the madness of a Trump presidency.

The book that every economist and any anchor on television should have when they speak about the global economy.

We are humans. We need to share. There is life beyond targets.

This does need a reminder.

Yes. We need a reminder that we are humans.

The Rich Man Vs The Average Joe

Why should the super rich get away with it ?

Make yourself heard. There are guys who earn 50 million, 100 million, 500 million a year. It cannot sit with them when the rest have to struggle. Make your voice heard.

Recession Fund. We now know now that recession is a part of capitalism. To mitigate it at a basic level everyone earning more than 10 million should payout 10% to this fund and those earning more than 100 million should pay out 20%. Imagine a guy earning 100 million dollars in that year. If he pays out 20 million he will be left with 80 million. It's hardly a dent; It doesn't make much of a difference to him. But a fund over the years can be damn useful. It should be left out of routine economic management. That fund should never be touched other than in the most distressed period, for basic human life. Capitalism needs a modification.

One of the most damning indictment of this system of economy is the rich poor divide. We need to share. As we are humans.

Wells Fargo makes us wonder about a cap on CEO salary or a rich mans tax; more so when the average Joe struggles.

CEO's in controversy rake it in... while the rich poor gap widens. Should there be more rich tax? Someone has $100 million when the rest cannot get essentials medicines?

It seems the CEO's win. Like they always do. To hell with the company.

But still let's not put a cap on what a person deserves. But let's put an expectation on what he shares.

I am against capping a CEO salary. Everyone should get the benefit of their ideas and talents. They should earn.

They should also learn to share what they earn. There have been saintly CEOs who have not taken a penny when their company was in trouble and there have been normal CEOs who have taken as much as they were entitled.

Which is alright. Perhaps you and I would have behaved normally too. But now its time to create a Share Fund. Because it's time to modify capitalism a bit, by including a bit of humanism.

THE FUTURE. IT'S UNPREDICTABLE.

The bad news points towards a recession and the good news in the other direction. But then maybe the positives outweigh the negatives and the bad news may manifest as problem areas and not as a full blown recession. How much effect has Trump had on this? The positives however are more in hope and expectations, more of work in process. While we wait for the negative effects of prolonged easy money QE, China excess, commodity bust, oil turning cheap and blasting the middle east and oil economies, the bank frauds and the Euro crisis; maybe we will be in the midst of a new technology wave and all these will best forgotten as history of the economy. Or will they resurface at an unexpected time as the ghost of a forgotten past more convoluted and more complicated. The Future...Its Unpredictable.

Trump has decisive ideas.1 trillion dollars spend to spur growth. He has proposed a corporate tax break. Tax breaks to corporates improves earnings, induces more investment, increases salaries and bonuses which in turn increases consumer and corporate spends. This will have domino effect and the result is an intended upswing. Retail sales showed upswing in Jan-2017 and labor market was positive. Health and drug cost to be cut, federal salaries capped.

China has tightened money policy and shows signs of having hit the bottom (called 'stabilizing').

Deutsche has scrapped bonuses to top employees for the second year and cut down on variable pay to select senior employees in an attempt to drastically reduce its costs.

On the other hand increased government spend will increase debt to above $ 20 trillion. Opposition may drag policy. The tax breaks may be diluted, may be postponed and may disappoint. Trump unable to manage senate and pass policies. Strong dollar will make exports costlier - hurts US exports. Trade wars (if it happens) will hammer globalization. The problems persist in Europe (bad banks, Brexit, Greece crisis and brittle Eurozone) - Japan and South American – Brazil, Mexico, Venezuela. South China Sea simmers, N Korea explodes and communities polarize.

But S-E Asia is a bright spot specially India which is now the fastest growing world economy.

Where will all this take us in 2017 and where will we all be by 2020.

2017-2020: The Unpredictable Future.

Last Quarter 2017: The Crash

2016: Carl Icahn made a 150% net short position on his portfolio. George Soros made a massive short in S&P 500.

Who will win? The Bulls or the Bears?

The Last Quarter of 2017...Oct 2017. Be Careful. The Ides of Mar − Apr 2017. The End Game of Oct - 2017.

Oct 2017: USA ?

Oct 2017: China, Japan. Shaky.

Oct 2017: India jolted But Stands Up to brave the Global Onslaught.

ONLY YOU CAN ACT.

Cause and effect. Indicators and outcome. This is an economic diagnosis done on the basis of an analysis of the symptoms.

AND YOU CAN ACT ONLY IF YOU KNOW.

"IN THE WOMB OF THE END LIES A NEW BEGINNING."

PIAM.

THE REVIVAL

Graphene. Bend anything.

Anti-ageing drugs. Live young forever.

Flying cars. Fly away.

Bye To All.

[156] Be Someone @The Revival.

A Recession Cannot Stop

The March Of Time

And

The Advance Of Technology.

THE TECH SHIFT

BY PIAM

2016 @ AMAZON * CREATESPACE

THE ADVENTURES OF THE ORANCZ TRIANGLEZ

PIAM CREATIONS

ANIMATION FILM @ 2017

pi.con.publisher@gmail.com

You Tube   The Piam Studio

Catch the Book: The Unpredictable Future - Live on You Tube

By Piam.

www.ingramcontent.com/pod-product-compliance
Lightning Source LLC
Chambersburg PA
CBHW071434180526
45170CB00001B/341